Math for Homeowners

Everyday Solutions

By William J. Saunders

ISBN-10: 1985763931
ISBN-13: 978-1985763937

Table of Contents

About This Book

It's amazing how many tasks and projects around
the house require math calculations. Sometimes
the basic formulas to make those calculations
aren't obvious or were forgotten. This book was
written to make many of them readily available,
and understandable.

But remember, the information is general and may
not apply to your situation. Consider that and
consider safety. Always consult with professionals
when in doubt, and / or when safety is involved.

Chapter 1   Air Quality

Too often, we take our indoor air for granted. Today's homes are sealed so much tighter than in the past that they breed and harbor unhealthy growths like mildew and mold, and trap all sorts of toxic fumes and allergens.

We have some measure of controlling the environment inside the home with intelligent hygienic practices, and the proper use of helpful appliances.

<u>Air Purifier</u>

Problem:
Concern about air pollution in the home suggests the need for an Air Purifier. Where to start?

Solution:
If the problem is in a room, a section, or the whole house, start by finding the Area of the space in Square Feet. Then shop for an Air Purifier of the appropriate size.

Length X Width = Area

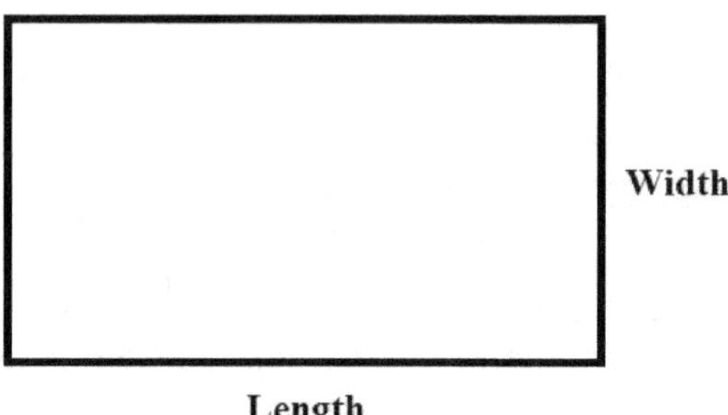

Example:
20 Feet Length X 15 Feet Width = Area of 300 Square Feet

Armed with the Area in Square Feet, the next consideration is Air Change per Hour (ACH).

A good bet, especially for allergy sufferers, is an Air Change per Hour (ACH) of 5 or more. Such an Air Purifier unit should change and filter the air in the specified space more than 5 times per Hour.

Dehumidifier

Problem:
The basement is damp and smells of mildew. You may also use an instrument such as a Hygrometer to measure Humidity.

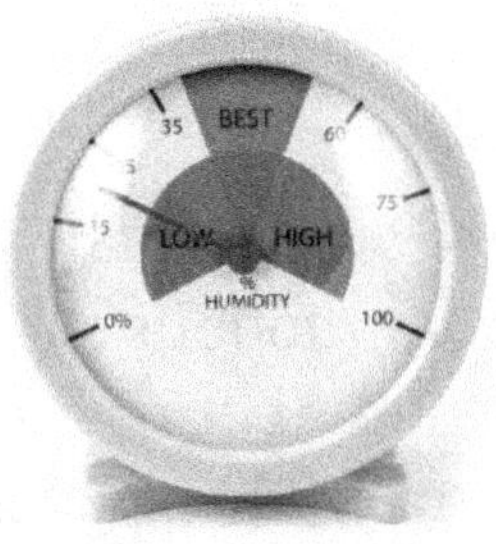

Hygrometer

Solution:
Use a dehumidifier of the appropriate size to remove some of the moisture from the air.
Start by determining the Area of the basement by multiplying the Length by the Width. This may be easier by measuring the exterior of the house if the plan is to dehumidify the entire basement.

Length X Width = Area

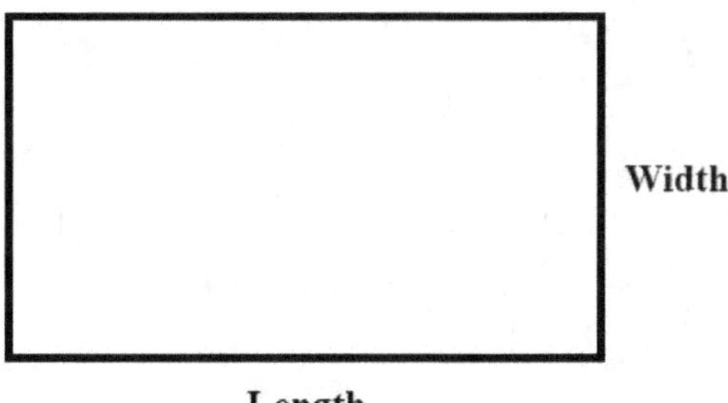

Example:

42 Feet Length X 24 Feet Width = 1,008 Square Feet Area

Next, evaluate the severity of the moisture in the space on a scale from moderate to wet. This will help to estimate the number of Pints of water per day to be removed from the space.

Examples:
Moderate: 1,000 Square Feet = 14 Pints per day
Very Wet: 1,000 Square Feet = 20 Pints per day

8 Pints = 4 Quarts = 1 Gallon

Check the dehumidifier specifications and choose according to the dampness of the space.

Reminder:
Dehumidifiers need a drain or must be manually emptied.

Humidifier

Problem:
Dry air in the home is causing respiratory irritation. Again, an instrument can be used to measure Humidity in the air.

Solution:
Increase moisture in the air with a humidifier of the right size.

Humidifiers typically come in four sizes: Small, Medium, Large, and Whole House based on the Area in Square Feet.

Determine the Area in Square Feet in which additional moisture is needed by multiplying the Length by the Width.

Area = Length X Width

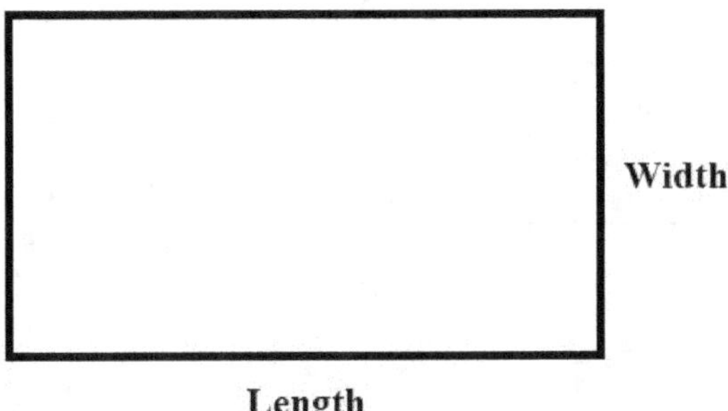

Examples:
20 Feet X 20 Feet = 400 Square Feet (Small)
25 Feet X 40 Feet = 1,000 Square Feet (Medium)
30 Feet X 50 Feet = 1,500 Square Feet (Large)
Optional: Whole House for forced air systems

Reminder:
Humidifiers need a water source or need to be hand filled.

1 Gallon = 4 Quarts = 8 Pints

<u>**Tools:**</u>

Tape Measure
Calculator
Hygrometer to measure humidity

Chapter 2   Carpentry

Carpentry is a science and involves all sorts of measurements, equations and formulas, not to mention numerous scales and tables.

Practical math around the house, whether for maintenance, improvement, or fun hobbies and projects, doesn't always have to be so demanding.

Problem:
Planning a project requires a materials list. What are some of the measurement details to consider?

Solution:

<u>Board Foot</u>

Often confused with the Length of a piece of wood, a Board Foot is actually a measure of Volume of a piece or pieces of wood,

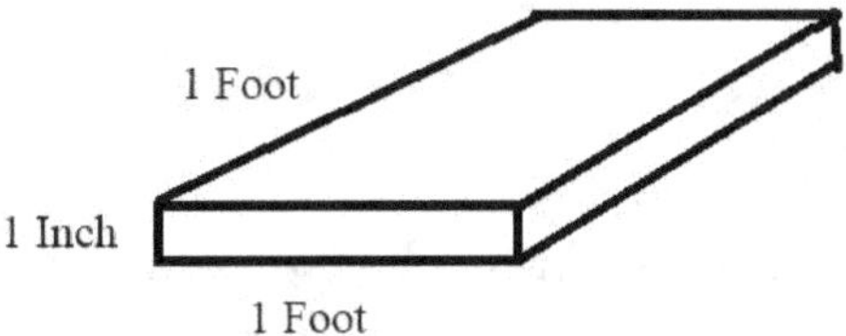

1 Board Foot = 1 Foot Wide X 1 Foot Long X 1 Inch Thick

Or

12 Inches Wide X 12 Inches Long X 1 Inch Thick / 144 = 1 Board Foot

Example 1:
A piece of wood 1 Foot Wide X 8 Feet Long X 1 Inch Thick = 8 Board Feet

Or

12 Inches Wide X 96 Inches Long X 1 Inch Thick / 144 = 8 Board Feet

Example 2:
A piece of wood 8 Inches Wide X 12 Feet Long X 2 Inches Thick is 16 Board Feet

Or

8 X 144 X 2 / 144 = 16 Board Feet

Linear Feet

This is the measurement typically used when buying wood for household projects. An 8 foot long board is an 8 long foot board, etc.

However, keep in mind that the actual Width and Thickness of a board is usually <u>NOT</u> the same as is advertised or specified.

For example:
A 2 X 4 piece of lumber is usually not 2 Inches X 4 Inches but more likely is 1 5/8 Inches X 3 1/2 Inches.
A 1 X 6 board is more likely 5/8 Inch X 5 1/2 Inches.

The smaller size is due to the waste caused by the sawing kerf waste at the manufacturing mill.

Keep these discrepancies in mind when planning a project and always measure before cutting. In fact, the old adage of "***Measure twice, cut once***" is a good practice.

<u>Miter Joints</u>

To bevel two parts to form a Right Angle Joint, the joining ends of the two beveled parts should add up to a 90 Degree angle.

Normally two 45 degree angles are used, though it can be any two angles that add up to 90 Degrees (30 + 60 = 90 Degrees, etc.).

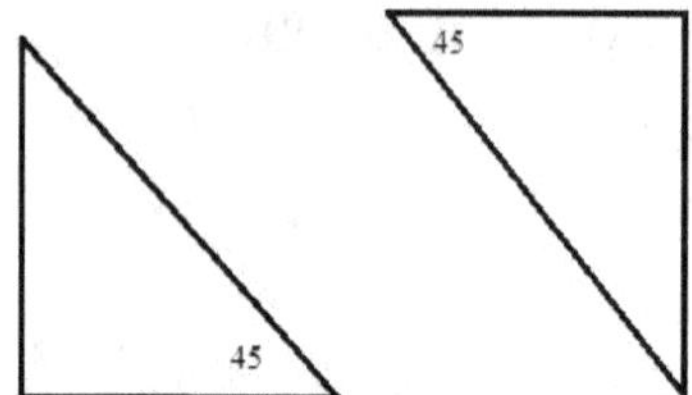

A 45 Degree Miter cut
(Miter joints are used for frames, pipes, molding
and much, more)

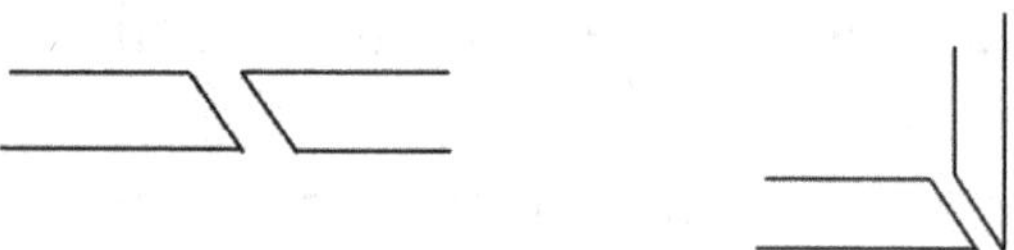

Cuts other than those with 45 Degree Bevel cuts
are sometimes needed and are also called Miter
Joints.

Examples:

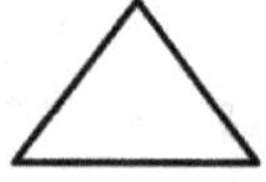

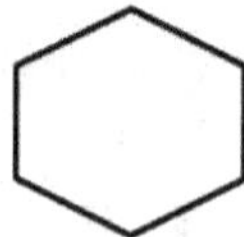

Note: When measuring and sawing, always be aware of the kerf (width of the saw blade) waste.

<u>Tools:</u>

Tape Measure
Protractor
Mitering Tools
Caliper

Chapter 3   Decimals

For various reasons, not the least of which is accuracy, Decimals are used instead of Fractions.

And sometimes when Fractions are used, they are the "nearest" Fraction to the Decimal (1/8 may be used to represent 0.124 instead of the more accurate 0.125).

Problem:
Many tools, accessories, and numerous other things are specified in either Fractions or their Decimal Equivalents, rarely both at the same time.

For example, a project might call for a hole of 0.125 Inch, a Decimal, but the drill bits are marked in Fractions. Which is the proper drill bit for the job?

Solution:

Convert the Decimal to a Fraction.
Numerator / Denominator

The Denominator depends on whether the Decimal is Tenths, Hundredths, or Thousandths: 10 for Tenths, 100 for Hundredths, or 1,000 for Thousandths.

The Numerator will be a multiple of 10 for Tenths, 100 for Hundredths, or 1,000 for Thousandths.

Numerator / Denominator

Examples:

Tenths:
The Decimal is 0.5
Multiply the Decimal by 10 for the Numerator
The Denominator is 10
Divide for the Fraction equivalent
0.5 = 5/10 = 1/2

Hundredths:
The Decimal is 0.25
Multiply the Decimal by 100 for the Numerator
The Denominator is 100
Divide for the Fraction equivalent
0.25 = 25/100 = 1/4

Thousandths:
The Decimal is 0.125
Multiply the Decimal by 1000 for the Numerator
The Denominator is 1000
Divide for the Fraction equivalent
0.125 = 125/1000 = 1/8

To convert a Fraction to a Decimal, divide the Numerator by the Denominator.

Numerator / Denominator

Examples:

1/8 = 0.125

1/4 = 0.25

1/2 = 0.5

The following table lists many of the standard Decimal Equivalents.

8ths	Dec	16ths	Dec	32nds	Dec	64ths	Dec	64ths	Dec
1/8	0.125	1/16	0.062	1/32	0.031	1/64	0.015	33/64	0.515
1/4	0.250	3/16	0.187	3/32	0.093	3/64	0.046	35/64	0.546
3/8	0.375	5/16	0.312	5/32	0.156	5/64	0.078	37/64	0.578
1/2	0.500	7/16	0.437	7/32	0.218	7/64	0.109	39/64	0.609
5/8	0.625	9/16	0.562	9/32	0.281	9/64	0.140	41/64	0.640
3/4	0.750	11/16	0.687	11/32	0.343	11/64	0.171	43/64	0.671
7/8	0.875	13/16	0.812	13/32	0.406	13/64	0.203	45/64	0.703
		15/16	0.937	15/32	0.468	15/64	0.234	47/64	0.734
				17/32	0.531	17/64	0.265	49/64	0.765
				19/32	0.593	19/64	0.296	51/64	0.796
				21/32	0.656	21/64	0.328	53/64	0.828
				23/32	0.718	23/64	0.359	55/64	0.859
				25/32	0.781	25/64	0.390	57/64	0.890
				27/32	0.843	27/64	0.421	59/64	0.921
				29/32	0.906	29/64	0.453	61/64	0.953
				31/32	0.968	31/64	0.484	63/64	0.984

Decimal Equivalents

Chapter 4   Electrical

As a rule, homeowners shouldn't do electrical work around the house without proper training, certification and / or expert guidance.

It is important though to be aware of the basics of the household electrical system, appliances and auxiliary components.

AC (Alternating Current) (House Current)

Electrical Outlets:

Problem:
How many appliances can be plugged into an outlet?

Solution:
It depends on the Power requirements of each appliance.

If the fuse or circuit breaker for that outlet is 15 Amperes on a 115 Volt line, and that is the only outlet on that circuit, then calculate as follows:

Current in Amperes X Voltage = Power in Watts
15 Amperes X 115 Volts = 1,725 Watts

Check the Wattage on each appliance and don't exceed 1,725 Watts at one time for that circuit.

If there is more than 1 outlet on the circuit, then proportion the distribution of the appliances accordingly:

Example: Five 60 Watt Light Bulbs plus a 100 Watt TV uses 400 Watts on a circuit.

Problem:
The Fuse or Circuit Breaker box shows that the whole house has 200 Amperes available. How many Watts is that?

Solution:
Power in Watts = Amperes X Voltage
200 Amperes X 115 Volts = 23,000 Watts maximum for the whole house.

23,000 Watts = 23 Kilowatts (kW)

Keep in mind, however, that some appliances use a higher voltage (220 – 240 volts) such as stoves, ovens, water heaters, furnaces, and others. Consequently, they will also use more Power and need to be considered when evaluating the total household Current needs.

Power (Watts) = Current (Amperes) X Voltage (Volts)

Wire, Bulbs, or Fuses

Problem:
Can current flow through a wire, bulb, or fuse, or is it an open / broken circuit?

Solution:
Disconnect or remove wire, bulb, or fuse from any <u>disconnected</u> circuit.
Check continuity using a Multimeter.
Set to Ohms (Ω) (X1K) on this Multimeter.

On the Ohms Scale above, Zero (0) is on the right side and Infinity (∞) is on the left side.

Touch one probe to each end of the wire or each contact of the fuse **while they are disconnected from any circuit**.

A Zero (0) reading means there is continuity (Current can flow) and an Infinity (∞) reading usually means the circuit is broken (open).

Extension Cords

Be aware that one size doesn't fit all uses. Extension Cords vary in length, capacity, environmental capabilities indoor, outdoor, waterproofing, etc.), and more.

When selecting an Extension Cord for a particular purpose, be aware of the Power needs of the unit requiring the Power and the capacity of the source.

For example:

If the unit to be Powered requires 10 Watts, the Extension Cord must be able to deliver 11.5 Amperes of Current.

Current = Voltage / Power
115 Volts / 10 Watts = 11.5 Amperes needs to be delivered through the Extension Cord.

A typical household circuit delivers 15 Amperes to the Outlets on that circuit. So if there is only 1 Outlet on the circuit, 15 Amperes is available at that Outlet to feed the Extension Cord.

The next consideration is the Extension Cord length needed to reach the unit to be Powered. Resistance in the Extension Cord reduces the Current flow, so whereas a 6 feet long Extension Cord may suffice to Power a unit 4 feet away from the source, a 50 feet long Extension Cord of the same Current-carrying capacity might not.

Instead, a heavier Gauge Extension Cord may be needed to prevent overheating and / or blowing a fuse or tripping a circuit breaker.

Length	to 10 Amps	to 15 Amps
to 25 Feet	16 Gauge	14 Gauge
to 50 Feet	16 Gauge	14 Gauge
to 75 Feet	14 Gauge	12 Gauge
to 100 Feet	14 Gauge	12 Gauge

Also be aware that most houses are wired with 14 Gauge wire and have limited power handling capability. So while everything makes sense with the Extension Cord capacity, there has to be sufficient Power available at the source (Outlet).

Typical References:
Current: Amperes (Amps), Milliamp (.001 Amp)
Voltage: Volts
Power: Watts,
Kilowatt (kW) = 1,000 Watts (W)
Resistance: Ohms (R) (Ω)

<u>DC (Direct Current) (Batteries)</u>

Problem:
Is a battery good or bad?
Solution:
Test it using a Multimeter set to DC and a Range
above the Battery voltage specification.

Using a Multimeter like the one above, the DC
Range on the left side or the BATT Range at the
bottom could be used, depending on the Battery.

For example:

For a 1 1/2 Volt AA Battery, use either the BATT
Range and the 1.5 Scale, or the DC Range and the
2.5 Scale, then read the scale to see if the Battery
tests good.

For a 6 Volt Battery, use the DC Range and the
10 Volt Scale.

Typical References:

Current: Amperes (Amps), Milliamps (.001 Amp)
Voltage: Volts (V)
Power: Watts (W)
Resistance: Ohms (R) (Ω)
Infinity (∞)

<u>Tools:</u>

Multimeter
Calculator

<u>WARNING</u>:

**Consult a Licensed Electrician before touching
electrical circuits or components, or making
electrical decisions.**

Chapter 5 Flooring

Buying and installing Flooring in a home requires more consideration than just type and color or pattern. And more than price and warranty are important.

Often overlooked are the doors, the appliances, the stairs, and more. Lack of planning for Thickness is liable to cause many problems sooner or later.

Doors have to swing. Appliances have to fit. Stairs have to have safe footing. Math calculations can help.

Problem:
When considering new Flooring in a room, what math is involved?

Solution:
In addition to Area measurements, the Thickness of the material is often overlooked when choosing and can become a problem later.

Following are some different Flooring choices and the measurements to bear in mind.

First, get the dimensions (Length and Width to find the Area) of the room or space.

The Area in Square Feet or Square Yards is the Product of the Length times the Width of the space to be carpeted.

Length X Width = Area

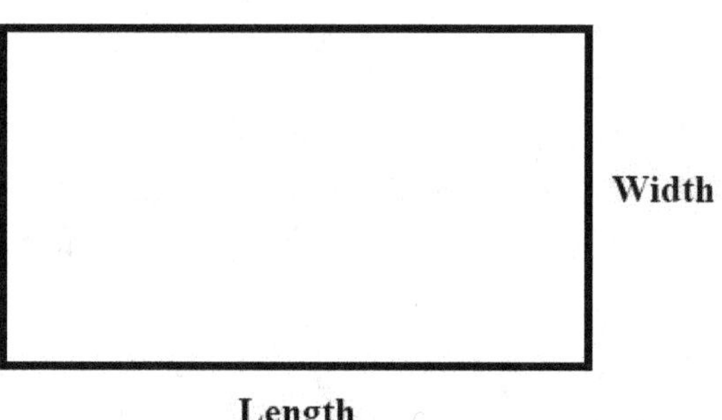

Example:

15 Feet in Long X 12 Feet Wide = 180 Square Feet

To convert that to Square Yards, divide by 9
(9 Square Feet = 1 Square Yard)

180 Square Feet / 9 = 20 Square Yards

Carpet:

When considering Carpet for the space, check the Thickness of the Carpet's pile and the Thickness of the Padding. Doors that swing into the room may need to be adjusted or trimmed, and that may not be practical or economical, or may result in intolerable drafts.

Example:
The bottom of a Door may be 1 Inch above the floor.
The Carpet Pile may be 3/4 Inch thick and the Padding below the carpet may add another 7/16 Inch to the total thickness.

3/4 Inch + 7/16 Inch = 1 3/16 Inch
(3/4 = 12/16 + 7/16 = 19/16 = 1 3/16)

So in this case the Door or Doors will have to be adjusted or trimmed to be operational. How will that affect the Door Threshold?

Alternatives include selecting thinner Pile, thinner Padding, or a different type of Flooring.

Laminate:

The thickness of Laminate Flooring varies as does the Thickness of the Underlayment that supports the Flooring.

Often, the thickness is specified in Millimeters rather than in Inches.

1 Inch = 25.4 Millimeters
1 Millimeter = 0.04 Inch

Tile:

Depending on the material, Tiles might be as much
as 1/2 Inch Thick to as Thin as 1/8 Inch. Add to
that the Backer Board (1/4 or 1/2 Inch) and, if
needed, a wood subfloor.

Wood:

Typical Hardwood Flooring is 3/4 Inch Thick plus
whatever subfloor or underlayment will be used.

Tools:

Tape Measure
Calculator

Chapter 6   Fluids

Liquid measure differs from Dry measure in various ways. Don't confuse a Liquid Ounce and an Ounce of Weight, for example.

Problem:
A plant treatment product calls for 2 Tablespoons of product per 1 Gallon of water. How much product is the proper amount for 16 Ounces of water?

Solution:
Given that 1 Gallon = 128 Ounces
And
2 tablespoons = 1 Ounce
Proceed as follows:

Convert the 1 Gallon:
128 Ounces /16 Ounces = 8 or 1/8 of 128
So
16 Ounces is 1/8 of a Gallon

Convert the 2 Tablespoons (which is 1 Ounce):
1 Ounce / 8 = 0.125 Ounce = 1/8 Ounce
So
1/8 of an Ounce

Therefore the proportion is 1/8 Ounce (0.125) of product per 16 Ounces of water

Further:
Per the Liquid Measurement Chart,
1 Teaspoon = 1/6 (0.167) Ounce
So 1/8 (0.125) / 1/6 (0.167) = 3/4 (0.75) Teaspoon

In this case, the proper mixture is also 3/4
Teaspoon of product per 16 Ounces of water.

Liquid Measurement Chart

1 Gallon = 4 Quarts = 8 Pints = 128 Ounces
1 Quart = 2 Pints = 32 Ounces
1 Pint = 16 Ounces
8 Ounces = 1 Cup
1 Ounce = 2 Tablespoons
1 Tablespoon = 1/2 Ounce
1 Tablespoon = 3 Teaspoons
1 Teaspoon = 1/6 Ounce (approx.)
1 Ounce = 600 Drops (approx.)
1 Teaspoon = 100 Drops (approx.)

<u>Tools:</u>

Measuring Spoons and Cups
Eyedropper
Calculator

Chapter 7 Formulas and Equations

Where an Equation is an Expression recognized by an Equal (=) sign, a Formula is a Process or set of Instructions (like a recipe) that may contain Equations.

Circles

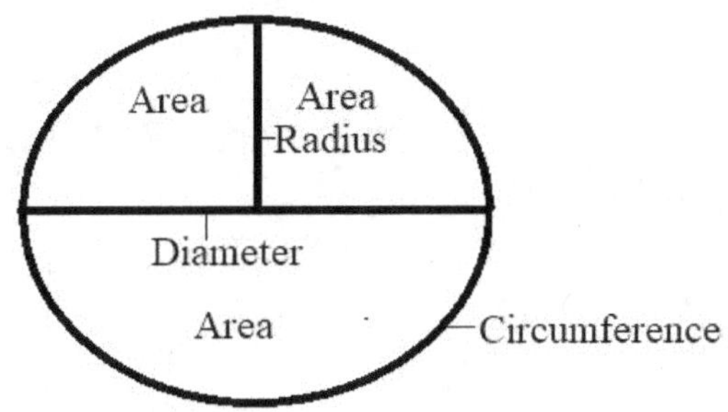

Find Area (A) $A = \pi R^2$
Find Circumference (C) $C = \pi D$
Find Diameter (D) $D = C / \pi$
Find Radius (R) $R = D / 2$
Find Radius (R) $R = C / 2 \pi$
Pi (π) $\pi = 3.14$ (rounded)

Rectangles

Square Inches = Length X Width
Square Feet = Length X Width

Square Foot = 144 Square Inches
Square Yards = Length X Width
Square Yard = 9 Square Feet

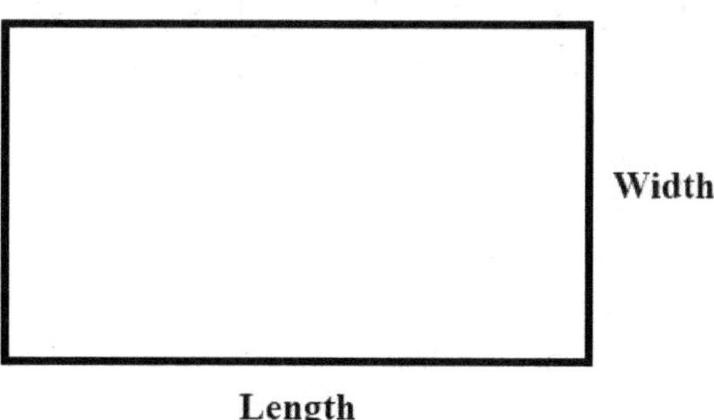

Triangles

Area = Height X Base / 2

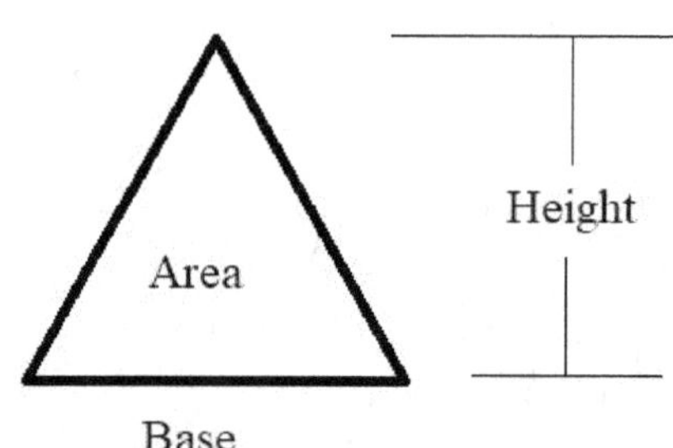

Linear Measurements

1 Foot	12 Inches
1 Yard	3 Feet
1 Mile	5,280 Feet
1 Mile	1,760 Yards

Cubic Measurements (Volume)

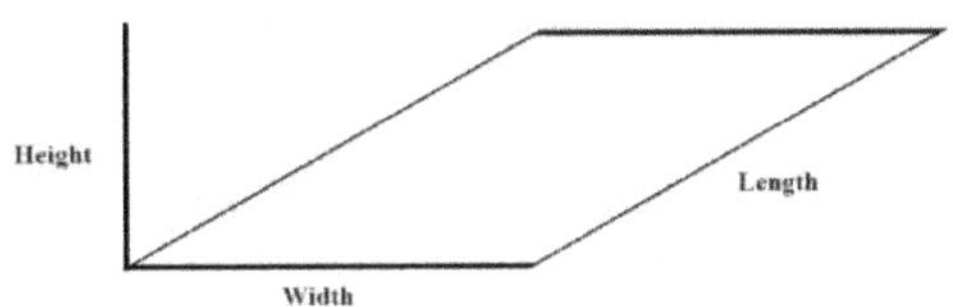

Length X Width X Height

1 Cubic Foot	1728 Cubic Inches
1 Cubic Yard	27 Cubic Feet

Liquid Measurements

1 Teaspoon	1/3 Tablespoon
1 Tablespoon	1/2 Ounce
1 Cup	8 Ounces
1 Pint	16 Ounces
1 Quart	32 Ounces
1 Gallon	128 Ounces

Tools:

Calculator
Protractor
Ruler
Tape Measure

Chapter 8   Fractions

A Fraction, representing a number between Zero
(0) and One (1), is composed of a Numerator (the
Dividend on top) and the Denominator (the
Divisor on bottom) (1/8, 1/4, 1/2, etc.).

When the Numerator is divided by the
Denominator the result is called the Quotient, a
Decimal. $(1/2 = 0.5)$

Problem:
Many tools, accessories, and numerous other
things are specified in either Fractions or their
Decimal Equivalents, rarely both at the same time.

For example, a project might call for a hole of
0.125 Inch. The drill bits are marked in Fractions.
Which is the proper drill bit for the job?

Solution:
Convert the Fraction to a Decimal or the Decimal
to a Fraction.

To convert a Fraction to a Decimal, divide the
Numerator by the Denominator.

Numerator / Denominator

1/8 = 0.125

1/4 = 0.25

1/2 = 0.5

Converting a Decimal to a Fraction:

Numerator / Denominator

The Denominator depends on whether the Decimal is Tenths, Hundredths, or Thousandths: 10 for Tenths, 100 for Hundredths, or 1,000 for Thousandths.
The Numerator will be a multiple of 10 for Tenths, 100 for Hundredths, or 1,000 for Thousandths.

Examples:

Tenths:
The Decimal is 0.5
Multiply the Decimal by 10 for the Numerator
The Denominator is 10
Divide for the Fraction equivalent
0.5 = 5/10 = 1/2

Hundredths:
The Decimal is 0.25
Multiply the Decimal by 100 for the Numerator
The Denominator is 100

Divide for the Fraction equivalent
0.25 = 25/100 = 1/4

Thousandths:
The Decimal is 0.125
Multiply the Decimal by 1000 for the Numerator
The Denominator is 1000
Divide for the Fraction equivalent
0.125 = 125/1000 = 1/8

The following table lists many of the standard
Decimal Equivalents.

Decimal Equivalents

8ths	Dec	16ths	Dec	32nds	Dec	64ths	Dec	64ths	Dec
1/8	0.125	1/16	0.062	1/32	0.031	1/64	0.015	33/64	0.515
1/4	0.250	3/16	0.187	3/32	0.093	3/64	0.046	35/64	0.546
3/8	0.375	5/16	0.312	5/32	0.156	5/64	0.078	37/64	0.578
1/2	0.500	7/16	0.437	7/32	0.218	7/64	0.109	39/64	0.609
5/8	0.625	9/16	0.562	9/32	0.281	9/64	0.140	41/64	0.640
3/4	0.750	11/16	0.687	11/32	0.343	11/64	0.171	43/64	0.671
7/8	0.875	13/16	0.812	13/32	0.406	13/64	0.203	45/64	0.703
		15/16	0.937	15/32	0.468	15/64	0.234	47/64	0.734
				17/32	0.531	17/64	0.265	49/64	0.765
				19/32	0.593	19/64	0.296	51/64	0.796
				21/32	0.656	21/64	0.328	53/64	0.828
				23/32	0.718	23/64	0.359	55/64	0.859
				25/32	0.781	25/64	0.390	57/64	0.890
				27/32	0.843	27/64	0.421	59/64	0.921
				29/32	0.906	29/64	0.453	61/64	0.953
				31/32	0.968	31/64	0.484	63/64	0.984

Chapter 9   Hardware

Planning a project, in addition to plans, includes a materials list. Nails, Screws and other Hardware are usually listed, but sometimes the items aren't itemized by size (Length, Width, Gauge, Type, or other specification needed to purchase the correct part).

<u>Nails</u>

Problem:
Which Nails and Screws are needed for a project?

Solution:
Most small Nails are sized by length and wire Gauge (Diameter). The higher the Gauge number, the thinner the Nail. In parts of the world Nails are sized in Millimeters, but in the U.S. they are usually sized in Pennies, or d (for denarius, a penny-like Roman coin) (for example, 4d, 5d, 6d, etc. are different lengths).

Penny Nails	
d	**Inches**
2	1
3	1 1/4
4	1 1/2
5	1 3/4
6	2
7	2 1/4
8	2 1/2
9	2 3/4
10	3
12	3 1/4
16	3 1/2
20	4
30	4 1/2
40	5
50	5 1/2
60	6
70	7
80	8

Penny Nails

Nail Gauge

The Gauge and "d" values go in opposite directions.

Example:
12d, 15d and 20d = 9, 8, and 6 gauge respectively.

Gauge	12 1/2	12 1/2	11 1/2	11 1/2	10 1/4	10 1/4	9	9	8	6	5	4	3	2
Inches														
1														
1 1/4														
1 1/2	4d													
1 3/4		5d												
2			6d											
2 1/4				7d										
2 1/2					8d									
2 3/4						9d								
3							10d							
3 1/4								12d						
3 1/2									16d					
3 3/4														
4										20d				
4 1/4														
4 1/2											30d			
4 3/4														
5												40d		
5 1/4														
5 1/2													50d	
5 3/4														
6														60d

Nail Chart

Gauge	Inch	Millimeter
2	0.2625	6.668
2 1/2	0.253	6.43
3	0.2437	6.19
3 1/2	0.234	5.94
4	0.2253	5.723
4 1/2	0.216	5.49
5	0.207	5.258
5 1/2	0.2	5.08
6	0.192	4.877
6 1/2	0.184	4.67
7	0.177	4.496
7 1/2	0.17	4.32
8	0.162	4.115
8 1/2	0.155	3.94
9	0.1483	3.767
9 1/2	0.142	3.61
10	0.135	3.429
10 1/2	0.128	3.25
11	0.1205	3.061
11 1/2	0.113	2.87
12	0.1055	2.68
12 1/2	0.099	2.51

Wire Gauge Chart

Screws

#	Diameter
0	1/16
1	5/64
2	3/32
3	7/64
4	7/64
5	1/8
6	9/64
7	5/32
8	5/32
9	11/64
10	3/16
11	13/64
12	7/32
14	1/4
16	17/64
18	19/64
20	5/16

Wood Screw Chart

Number	Diameter	Fraction	UNC	UNF
0	0.06	1/16		80
1	0.07	5/64	64	72
2	0.08	3/32	58	64
3	0.09	7/64	48	56
4	0.11	7/64	40	48
5	0.12	1/8	40	44
6	0.13	9/64	32	40
8	0.16	5/32	32	36
10	0.19	3/16	24	32
12	0.21	7/32	24	28
14	0.24	1/4	20	28
5/16	0.31	5/16	18	24
3/8	0.37	3/8	16	24

Machine Screws

UNC = Coarse Threads per Inch

UNF = Fine Threads per Inch

Pilot Holes

Before hammering in a Nail or driving a Screw,
it's usually a good idea to drill a Pilot Hole to
prevent splitting and for easier inserting.
Determine the Diameter of the Screw or Nail and
drill a smaller Diameter Pilot Hole.

Tools:

Hammers
Assorted Screwdrivers
Caliper
Drill and Bits

Chapter 10   HVAC

HVAC is a catch-all acronym for Heating, Ventilation and Air Conditioning. The Heating and Air Conditioning are often represented in BTU's.

BTU stands for British Thermal Unit and is based on the amount of heat that will melt 2,000 Pounds (1 Ton) of ice in 24 Hours from the days of solid ice being in common use but, more accurately, the amount of heat required to raise One (1) Pound of liquid water one (1) Degree Fahrenheit.

In Heating BTU refers to the amount of heat generated. In Air Conditioning it refers to the amount of heat removed.

Problem:
What size air conditioner is needed for a given space?

Solution:

Air Conditioner (Room)

Measure the space:
Length and Width

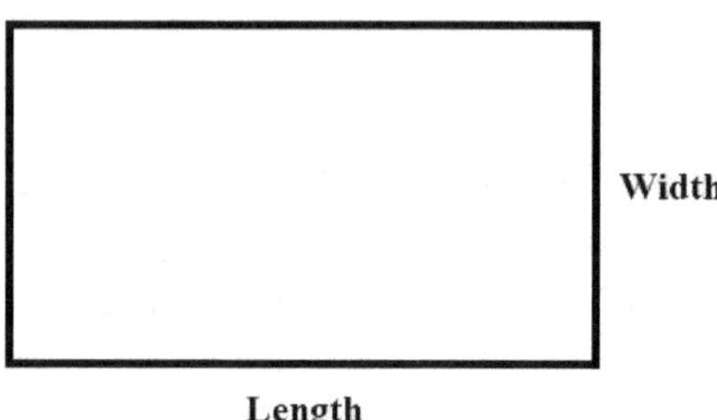

Multiply the Length by the Width
Then multiply by 25 BTU

Length X Width X 25 BTU
Example:

12 Feet X 18 Feet X 25 = 5,400 BTU (1/2 Ton)

A 1 Ton Air Conditioner = 12,000 BTU

Air Conditioning System (Whole House)

Measure each room and add the measurements together:

Total Length X Width X 25 BTU

Example:

40 Feet X 23 Feet X 25 = 23,000 BTU (2 Tons)

A 1 Ton Air Conditioner = 12,000 BTU

These are general rules-of-thumb for estimating HVAC needs, typically for rooms with standard 8 Foot ceilings.

Air Conditioner Efficiency Rating

SEER is the acronym for Seasonal Energy Efficiency Ratio and is a measure of the efficiency of an Air Conditioner.

Example:

A 5,000 BTU Air Conditioner
It runs 10 Hours per Day for 120 Days
It has a SEER Rating of 10

5,000 BTU per Hour X 10 Hours per Day X 120 Days = 6,000,000 BTU's per Year

6,000,000 BTU's per Year / 10 SEER Rating = 600,000 Watt Hours per Year (600 Kilowatt Hours per Year) (1 Kilowatt Hour = 1,000 hours)

If the cost per Kilowatt Hour is $0.30 then the average cost per year to run this Air Conditioner is:
600 Kilowatt Hours X $0.30 = $180

Air Change per Hour (ACH)

Problem:
What Air Change rate is needed for a room?

Solution:
Determine the room area by multiplying the room Length by the Width.

Example:

15 Feet Length X 15 Feet Width = 225 Square Feet Area
Using this Area figure, buyers make their decision using the room air conditioner specifications.

Professionals usually include the Height of the room to get the Cubic feet (Length X Width X Height = Cubic Feet Volume. Then they use the Cubic Feet per Minute (CFM) to determine the Air Change per Hour rate (ACH).

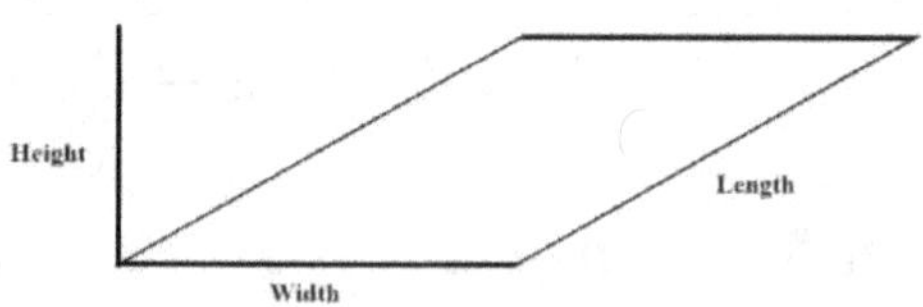

CFM X 60 Minutes / Volume in Cubic Feet = ACH

A good choice for the average room is 5 to 8 ACH.

Tools:

Tape Measure
Calculator

Chapter 11   Insulation

It's interesting to find how few people do anything about Insulating their attics to prevent a lot of their expensive heat to be drawn up there.

Some have never even ventured into the attic, while others are satisfied with an inch or so of some scattered material.

This book won't go into the various types of insulation but will give a brief overview of the measurements that are important when choosing to insulate.

Problem:

How much Insulation should be in the floor of an attic?

Solution:

Begin by measuring the Length and the Width of the space to be Insulated to get the Area in Square Feet. It may be practical to measure from the outside of the house, depending on the type of house and attic.

Length in Feet X Width in Feet = Area in Square Feet

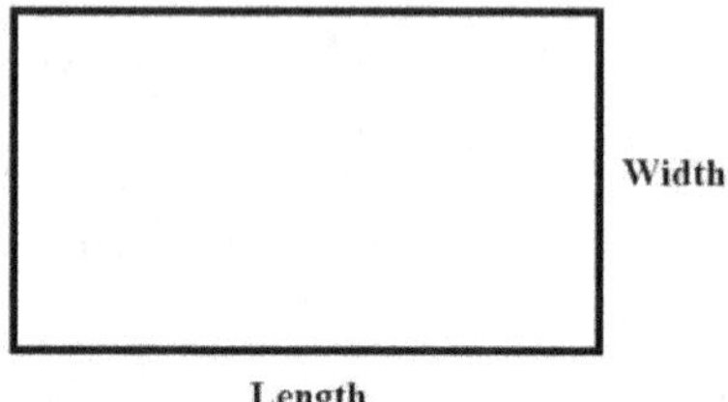

Example:

40 Feet Long X 25 Feet Wide = 1,000 Square Feet

R-Value

R-Value is a measure of resistance to heat flow and is used to describe most Insulation.

The Depth of the Insulation is one way to estimate the R-Value in or for your attic. Typically, Insulation below or up to 8 Inch attic floor Joists has an R-Value of up to R-21. The recommended R-Value for Southern Climates is R-38 at about 14 Inches, and for Northern Climates it's R-49 at about 17 Inches.

The higher the R Value the more effective it will be as an Insulator.

Tools

Tape Measure

Chapter 12   Landscaping

There are dozens of things around the exterior of the home that require math calculations. The most obvious is the lawn and the numerous products used to keep it healthy and attractive (fertilizer, sod, seed, lime, pesticide, etc.).

Additionally, numerous projects from gardens to decks to patios will also require measurements.

Problem:
How much lawn care product is needed for a task?

Solution:
Spreading seed, fertilizer, lime and other products on a lawn is usually a matter of determining the Area in Square Feet to be covered.

Area in Square Feet = Length in Feet X Width in Feet

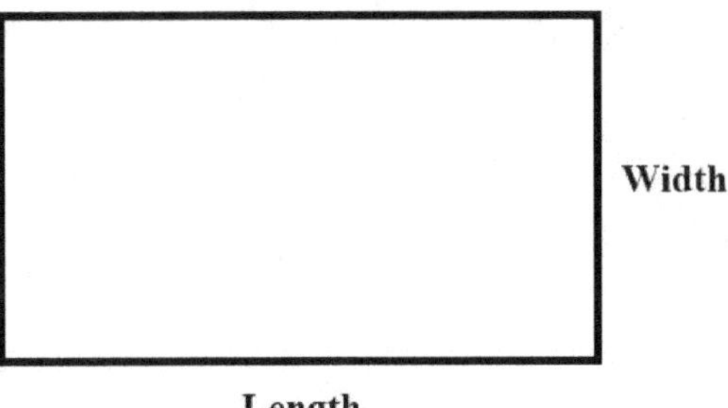

Instructions on the product bag or container will explain methods, cautions and coverage.

When spreading Liquid products, the same Area dimensions are needed, but Liquid measures are also required. Often the liquid product is diluted in water, so a refresher on Liquid measure will be helpful.

1 Gallon = 4 Quarts = 8 Pints = 128 Ounces
1 Quart = 2 Pints = 32 Ounces
1 Pint = 16 Ounces
8 Ounces = 1 Cup
1 Ounce = 2 Tablespoons
1 Tablespoon = 1/2 Ounce
1 Tablespoon = 3 Teaspoons
1 Teaspoon = 1/6 Ounce (approx.)
1 Ounce = 600 Drops (approx.)
1 Teaspoon = 100 Drops (approx.)

Weight

1 pound = 16 Dry Ounces

Firewood

Problem:

How much firewood is in a Cord?

Solution:
1 Cord of wood = 4 Feet High X 8 Feet Long X 4 Feet Deep

Buying firewood by the Cord is usually more economical than buying in small bundles. The actual dimensions of the Cord will vary by cut size (2 Foot Long logs, 3 Foot Long logs, etc.) and whether dumped by truck or stacked.

Stone

Problem:
How does one decide how much stone is required for a project?

Solution:
When estimating how much Stone will be needed for a driveway, walkway, or as an underlayment for a shed or patio, think in terms of Cubic Feet, Cubic Yards, and Tons.

Square Feet = Length in Feet X Width in Feet

Cubic Feet = Length in Feet X Width in Feet X Depth or Height in Feet

9 Square Feet = 1 Square Yard

27 Cubic Feet = 1 Cubic Yard

Square Yards = Length in Yards X Width in Yards

Cubic Yards = Length in Yards X Width in Yards X Depth or Height in Yards

1 Ton = 2,000 Pounds

In deciding how many tons might be required, measure the Area in Square Feet and the Depth or Height in Inches.

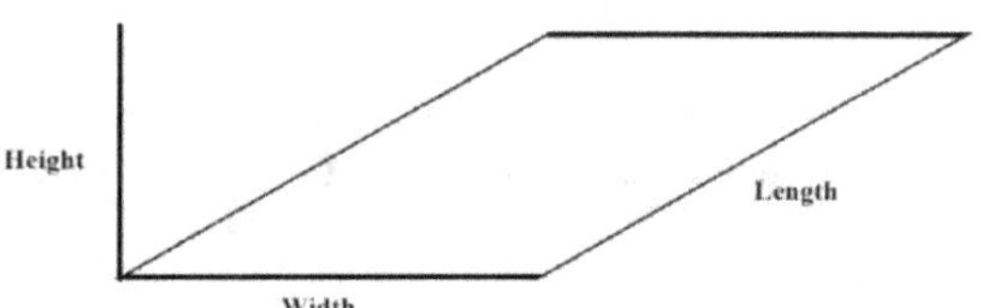

The Depth will determine Cubic Feet, Yards, or Tons by the type and size of the stone or gravel, which may be as small as pea size to large ragged stone. The supplier will have a chart to estimate the Cubic Feet, Yards or Tons required for the job.

If the project calls for a Circle instead of a Rectangle, find the Area using this Equation.

Area of a Circle = πR^2

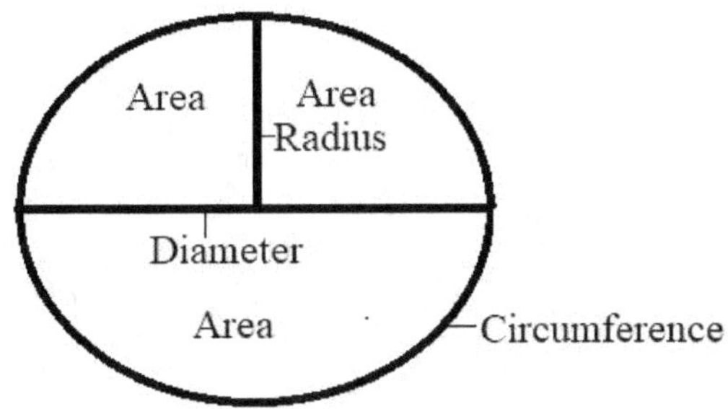

Where $\pi = 3.14$ (rounded)

Again, the supplier can aid with the Depth or Height depending on the material to be used.

Tools:

Tape Measure
Calculator
Shovel
Rake
Wheelbarrow
Gloves
Soil pH Tester

Chapter 13   Lighting

Output	Bulbs Energy Usage in Watts		
Lumens	Incandescent	LED	CFL
200	25	3	
450	40	8	13
800	60	13	15
1100	75	15	25
1600	100	20	30
2600	150	28	35

Actual values vary among products

LED = Light Emitting Diode

CFL = Compact Fluorescent Light

Chapter 14　　Metrics

While many projects or tasks require Standard measurements, more than a few will use Metrics. Some consider Metrics to be easier and more straightforward, while others think in terms of Standard dimensions and must convert one to the other by Equation or using a Conversion Table.

Problem:
How does one convert Inches to Centimeters?

Solution:
1 Inch = 2.54 Centimeters
And
1 Centimeter = 0.39 Inch

The following is a Metric Conversion Table:

Metric Conversion Table

Inches	Centimeters		Centimeters	Inches
1	2.54		1	0.39
2	5.08		2	0.79
3	7.62		3	1.18
4	10.16		4	1.57
5	12.70		5	1.97
6	15.24		6	2.36
7	17.78		7	2.76
8	20.32		8	3.15
9	22.86		9	3.54
Feet	Meters		Meters	Feet
1	0.30		1	3.28
2	0.61		2	6.56
3	0.91		3	9.84
4	1.22		4	13.12
5	1.52		5	16.40
6	1.83		6	19.69
7	2.13		7	22.97
8	2.44		8	26.25
9	2.74		9	29.53
Yards	Meters		Meters	Yards
1	0.91		1	1.09
2	1.83		2	2.19
3	2.74		3	3.28
4	3.66		4	4.37
5	4.57		5	5.47
6	5.49		6	6.56
7	6.40		7	7.66
8	7.32		8	8.75
9	8.23		9	9.84

1 Inch = 25.4 Millimeters
1 Millimeter = 0.04 Inch

Chapter 15　　Mortgage

Few people purchase a house for cash and must borrow some or the entire selling price. A Mortgage is the commonly used legal instrument in these transactions. It spells out the terms of repayment of the debt.

Problem:
What is Mortgage Amortization all about?

Solution:
Mortgages are the financing instruments most often used to purchase real estate. They commit that a certain sum of money plus a certain percentage of Interest will be repaid over a certain period of Time.

A typical Mortgage is for a term of 30 years during which time the debt is Amortized (paid off). In the beginning the Payments are mostly Interest with little going toward the reduction of the Principal. This ratio changes as time goes on so that toward the end of the term the Payments are mostly going toward the remainder of the Principal.

Example:

A $100,000 Mortgage at 10% Interest for 30 years

360 Monthly Payments @ $877.57

Payment #1
Interest = $833.33 Principal = $44.24

Payment #359
Interest = $14.48 Principal = $863.09

To arrive at these figures manually calculate the monthly Interest rate:

10% Interest / 12 months
10% = 0.10
0.10 / 12 = 0.008333333

Multiply the Principal Balance by the monthly Interest rate:

$100,000 X 0.008333333 = $833.33 Interest

Subtract the Interest from the Payment

$877.37 - $833.33 = $44 Principal (rounded off)

The new Principal Balance is now:

$100,000 - $44 = $99,956

Most **Automobile Loans** are similar in that the majority of the early Payments are Interest and very little goes toward repaying the Principal.

Tools:

Calculator

Chapter 16　　Painting

When most people set out on a Paint project the considerations are primarily color and whether to use water-based or oil-based Paint.

Quantity of Paint is often low on the list, which accounts for either a second trip to the Paint store for more, or extra that winds up in some household storage area. Proper measurements will help.

Problem:
How much Paint will be needed for a project?

Solution:
Like many projects around the house, Painting requires some math to determine how much to buy for the job.

Paint comes in various sized containers for many different applications but the average do-it-yourselfer uses Pints, Quarts, or Gallons for brush and roller jobs.

1 Pint = 16 Ounces
1 Quart = 32 Ounces
1 Gallon = 128 Ounces

The amount of Paint needed to cover a given area depends on the viscosity or thickness. The thicker the fluid the less surface it will cover. Most cans of Paint specify the average area of coverage in Square Feet.

Determine the area to be Painted by multiplying the Length by the Width, or Height by the Width, in Feet to determine the Area in Square Feet. Round off on the high side and allow for spillage and waste. It's better to have some Paint left over than to not have enough to finish the job.

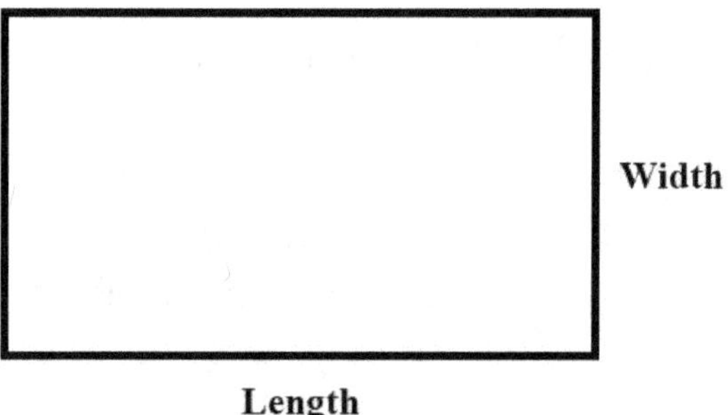

To Paint the walls of an interior room begin by measuring the Width of the four walls. Multiply that total by the Height (often 8 Feet).

Example:

11 + 13 + 11 + 13 = 48 X 8 = 384 total Square Feet

Measure the Width and Height of Doors and Windows to be subtracted from the total Square Feet.

The Door is 3 Feet X 7 Feet = 21 Square Feet

The Window is 5 Feet X 5 Feet = 25 Square Feet

Subtract 21 + 25 = 46 from 384 = 338 Square Feet to be Painted

The Paint specification shows 400 Square Feet per Gallon so one Gallon should do for one coat.

Some jobs will require two or more coats of Paint for adequate coverage. Factor that into the math calculations.

Similarly, cans of spray Paint will have typical coverage estimates specified in the directions on the Paint can label.

Tools:

Tape Measure
Painting Tools
Drop Cloths
Safety Glasses
Gloves

Chapter 17   Pool

Anyone with a swimming Pool knows that it either becomes a part time job to maintain it or an outsourcing expense.

Do-it-yourselfers need to know a good bit about math and chemistry to safely maintain their Pool. The following can help.

Problem:
Maintaining a Pool with chemicals takes some math to ensure proper dosages for cleanliness and for safety.

Solution:
The key measurement is the Volume of water in the Pool to apportion the products safely.

Volume of water in Cubic Feet = the Length of the Pool in Feet X the Width of the Pool in Feet X the average Depth of the Pool in Feet.

To calculate the average Depth of the water in a graduated Depth Pool (it has a shallow end and a deep end), draw a rectangle and a triangle (prism).

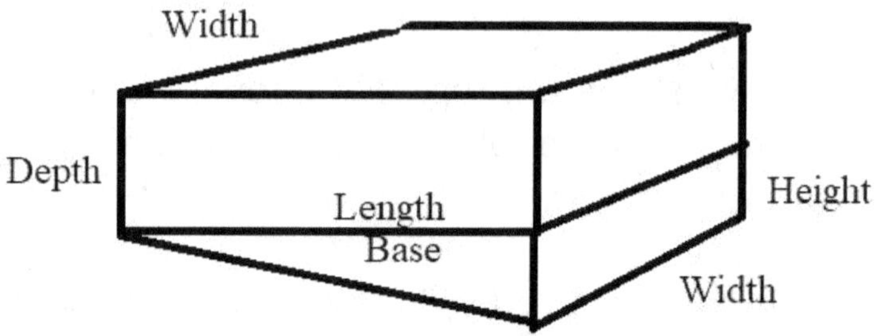

The rectangle will consist of the Length of the Pool by the Width of the Pool by the Depth of the Pool at the shallow end.

The triangle (prism) will consist of the Length of the Pool by the Width of the Pool by the Depth of the Pool at the deep end.

Example:

The Pool is 30 Feet in Length by 15 Feet in Width by 3 Feet in Depth at the shallow end to 8 Feet in Depth at the deep end.

The rectangle then is 30 Feet in Length by 15 Feet in Width by 3 Feet in Depth.

Rectangle Volume is Length X Width X Depth
30 Feet X 15 Feet X 3 Feet = 1,350 Cubic Feet

The triangle is 30 Feet in Length (Height of the triangle) by 15 Feet in Width (Width of the triangle) by 5 Feet in Depth (Base of the triangle).

Triangle Volume is Height X Width X Base / 2
30 Feet X 15 Feet X 5 Feet / 2 = 1,125 Cubic Feet

So the total Volume of water in this Pool, when properly full is 2,475 Cubic Feet.

1,350 + 1,125 = 2,475 Cubic Feet
Convert to Gallons of water:

1 Cubic Foot contains about 7.48 Gallons

2,475 Cubic Feet X 7.48 Gallons = 18,513 Gallons

Problem:
A Pool additive product calls for 2 Tablespoons of product per 1,000 Gallons of water. How much product is the proper amount for this Pool?

Solution:
Given that this Pool has 18,513 Gallons of water, and 2 Tablespoons = 1 Ounce use the following:

18,513 / 1,000 = 18.5
18.5 X 1 Ounce = 18.5 Fluid Ounces of product

pH

Pool Volume is needed to judge when and how much treatment is needed to maintain the preferred pH level of the water. Ideal pH is considered to be between 7.4 and 7.6.

Fluid Measure

1 Gallon = 4 Quarts = 8 Pints = 128 Ounces
1 Quart = 2 Pints = 32 Ounces
1 Pint = 16 Ounces
8 Ounces = 1 Cup
1 Ounce = 2 Tablespoons
1 Tablespoon = 1/2 Ounce
1 Tablespoon = 3 Teaspoons
1 Teaspoon = 1/6 Ounce (approx.)
1 Ounce = 600 Drops (approx.)
1 Teaspoon = 100 Drops (approx.)

Weight

1 Pound = 16 Dry Ounces

Tools:

Tape Measure
Calculator

Pool pH Testing Kit
Safety Glasses
Gloves

Chapter 18   Recipes

Whether you are a seasoned cook or a kitchen novice, there are times when a handy measurement Table or a reminder of an Equation can save time and maybe the day.

The following Tables and others in this book can save time and frustration. Happy Cooking!

Problem:
How does one properly measure items when following a food recipe?

Solution:

Liquid Measure Conversion Chart			
Dash =	< 1/4 Tsp		
1 Tbsp =	3 Tsp =	1/2 Fl Oz	
1/8 Cup =	1 Fl Oz =	1 Tbsp =	6 Tsp
1/4 Cup =	2 Fl Oz =	4 Tbsp =	12 Tsp
1/2 Cup =	4 Fl Oz =	8 Tbsp =	24 Tsp
1 Cup =	8 Fl Oz =	1/2 Pint =	237 Ml
2 Cups =	16 Fl Oz =	1 Pint =	474 Ml
4 Cups =	32 Fl Oz =	1 Quart =	946 Ml
2 Pints =	32 Fl Oz =	1 Quart =	0.964 L
1/4 Quart =	1/2 Pint =	1 Cup =	8 Fl Oz
1/2 Quart =	1 Pint =	2 Cups =	16 Fl Oz
4 Quarts =	128 Fl Oz =	1 Gallon =	3.78 L

Temperature Conversion	
Fahrenheit	Celsius
Degrees	Degrees
32	0
50	10
68	20
86	30
104	40
122	50
140	60
158	70
176	80
194	90
212	100
225	110
250	130
275	140
300	150
325	165
350	177
375	190
400	200
425	220
450	230
475	245
500	260

<u>Weight</u>

1 Pound = 16 ounces

<u>Tools</u>

Measuring Spoons and Cups
Scale
Calculator

Chapter 19   Roofing

Rarely is Roof installation or replacement a project a homeowner would undertake, it always good practice to understand some of the basic measurements that go into estimating the materials required and the potential cost.

Problem:
How to get a rough idea of a Roof size and how many Shingles might be needed.

Solution:
When considering a new Roof, it's best to be aware of what the <u>approximate</u> cost should or might be. To do that, some math calculations are needed.

Basically, Shingle estimates are measured in Squares and a Roofing Square is equal to 100 Square feet.

For a typical Gable Roof (an inverted V)

Gable Roof

Measure one side of the inverted V, which is a rectangle, and multiply the Length times the Width for the Area.

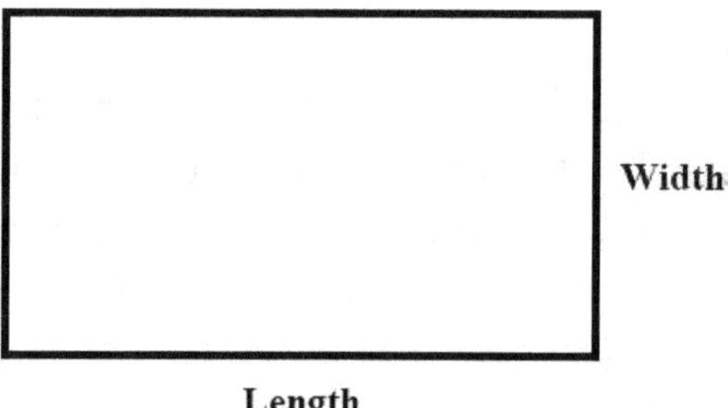

Area in Square Feet = Length X Width

Double that for both sides of the V.

Divide that by 100 to determine the number of Squares.

Example:
40 Feet X 30 Feet = 1200 X 2 = 2400 Square Feet
2400 / 100 = 24 Squares

Roof Pitch adds a bit more to the calculation.
Roof Pitch is the vertical rise in Inches for a 12
Inch horizontal distance.
For example, a 6/12 roof = a 6 Inch vertical rise in
a 12 Inch horizontal distance.

Roof Pitch	Multiplier
2/12	1.01
3/12	1.03
4/12	1.05
5/12	1.08
6/12	1.12
7/12	1.16
8/12	1.20
9/12	1.25
10/12	1.30
11/12	1.35
12/12	1.41
14/12	1.54
16/12	1.67
18/12	1.80
20/12	1.94
22/12	2.09
24/12	2.24

Roof Pitch Multiplier Table

Example:
A vertical rise of 6 Inches for a 12 Inch horizontal
distance (6/12) equates to a multiplier of 1.12.

So 24 Squares X 1.12 = 26.88 or 27 Squares.
Add 10% for waste = 30 Squares approximately.
In addition, these measurements plus perimeter
lengths will help determine other Roofing
materials that will add to the cost (underlayment,
drip edges, flashing, etc.

Other Roof styles (Hip, Mansard, etc. can get more
complicated to estimate, but when calculated by
sections (squares, rectangles, triangles) added
together, an approximation is still possible.

Tools:

Tape Measure
Calculator

Chapter 20   Sound System

Most shoppers for a Sound System are attracted by the Wattage of the product. Actually, the Wattage is far less important an indicator than is the Speaker Sensitivity Measurement expressed in Decibels. A good quality Speaker Sensitivity specification is 87 Decibels or above.

Consider the Table below:

Sound Measurements

What	Decibels
Jet Engine	140 +
Pain	125
Chain Saw	120
Lawn Mower	110
Train	95
City Traffic	85
Vacuum Cleaner	75
Refrigerator	55
Whisper	25

Now consider the Wattage driving a Speaker with an 87 Decibel Sensitivity Rating:

Power (Watts)	Volume (Decibels)
1	87
2	90
4	93
10	97
20	100
40	103
100	107
200	110

Wattage driving a Speaker with an 87 Decibel Sensitivity Rating

Doubling the Power in Watts increases the Volume by just 3 Decibels. So when looking for a good quality Sound System, Consider the Sensitivity rating in Decibels for the Speakers and the Output in Watts for the Amplifier.

Chapter 21   Sport

Running

Event	Miles	Meters	Yards
Sprints	.06, .12, .25	100, 200, 400	109, 219, 437
Middle	.5, .93	800, 1500	875, 1640
Long	1.86	3000	3281
5K	3.1	5000	5456
10K	6.2	10000	10912
1/2 Marathon	13.1	21082	182
1 Marathon	26.2	42164	365

Swimming

Event	Miles	Meters	Yards
50	0.03	50	55
100	0.06	100	109
200	0.12	200	219
400	0.25	400	417

Horse Racing

Event	Miles	Meters	Yards
Sprint	Under 8 Furlongs		
8 Furlongs	1	1609	1760
9 Furlongs	1/8	1811	1980
10 Furlongs	1 1/4	2012	2200
11 Furlongs	1 1/38	2213	2420
12 Furlongs	1 1/2	2414	2640

Chapter 22   Tools

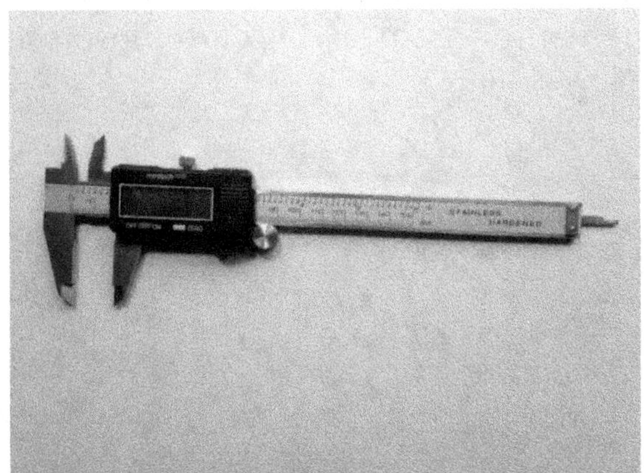

Caliper

Use the Caliper to measure inside and outside Diameter, and Depth. Some are switchable between Standard and Metric.

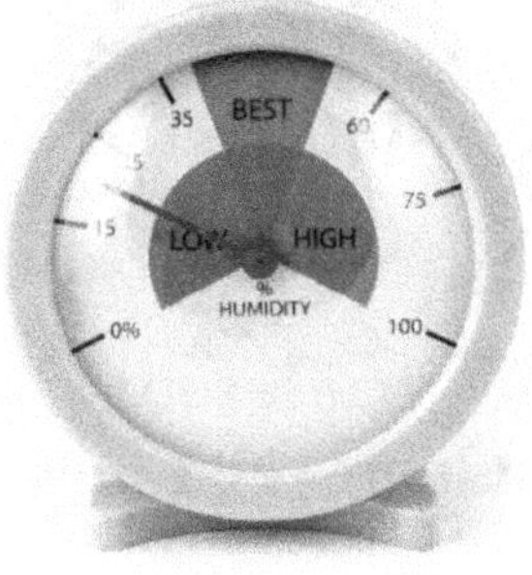

Hygrometer

Use a Hygrometer to measure Humidity

Measuring Spoons and Cups

Have a variety on hand for both outdoor work and in the kitchen for recipes. Discard those used for poisonous products.

Multimeter

Use the Multimeter to measure Volts (Batteries, etc.), Resistance (Ohms Ω), Continuity (0 - ∞), and Current (Amps).

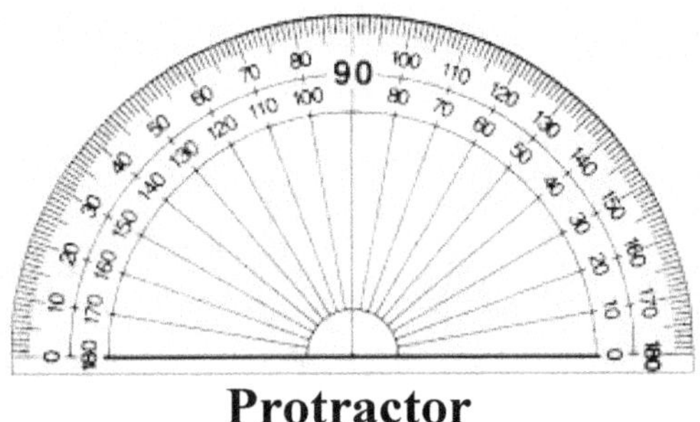

Protractor

Use the Protractor to check angles from 0 to 180
Degrees.

Tape Measure

It's good to have more than one Tape Measure
around the house. At the least have a 12 Feet and
a 25 Feet tape for convenience in measuring. They
are also available longer and shorter.

Chapter 23   Wind Chill

Wind MPH	Temperature Degrees F								
Calm	40	35	30	25	20	15	10	5	0
5	36	31	25	19	13	7	1	-5	-11
10	34	27	21	15	9	3	-4	-10	-16
15	32	25	19	13	6	0	-7	-13	-19
20	30	24	17	11	4	-2	-9	-15	-22
25	29	23	16	9	3	-4	-11	-17	-24
30	28	22	15	8	1	-5	-12	-19	-26
35	28	21	14	7	0	-7	-14	-21	-27
40	27	20	13	6	1	-8	-15	-22	-29
45	26	19	12	5	-2	-9	-16	-23	-30
50	26	19	12	4	-3	-10	-17	-24	-31
55	25	18	11	4	-3	-11	-18	-25	-32
60	25	17	10	3	-4	-11	-18	-26	-33

Wind Chill Chart

# Chapter 24	Wind Speed

Wind Speed			
MPH	KPH	Knots	Beaufort Scale
5	8	4.3	Light Breeze
10	16.1	8.7	Gentle Breeze
15	24.1	13	Moderate Breeze
20	32.2	17.4	Fresh Breeze
25	40.2	21.7	Strong Breeze
30	48.3	26.1	Strong Breeze
35	56.3	30.4	Near Gale
40	64.4	34.8	Gale
45	72.4	39.1	Gale
50	80.5	43.4	Strong Gale
55	88.5	47.8	Storm
60	96.6	52.1	Storm
65	104.6	56.5	Violent Storm
70	112.7	60.8	Violent Storm
75	120.7	65.2	Hurricane

Miles per Hour (MPH) to Kilometers per Hour (KPH) to Knots

Wind Speed			
Knots	KPH	MPH	Beaufort Scale
5	9.3	5.8	Light Breeze
10	18.5	11.5	Gentle Breeze
15	27.8	17.3	Moderate Breeze
20	37.1	23	Fresh Breeze
25	46.3	28.8	Strong Breeze
30	55.6	34.5	Near Gale
35	64.9	40.3	Gale
40	74.1	46	Gale
45	83.4	51.8	Strong Gale
50	92.7	57.5	Storm
55	101.9	63.3	Storm
60	111.2	69	Violent Storm
65	120.5	74.8	Hurricane

Knots to
Kilometers per Hour (KPH) to
Miles per Hour (MPH)

Warning

Always consult with professionals.

The information in this book is general.

Other factors can come into play.

Author

Some other books by William J Saunders
Available on Amazon.com

How to Buy New Windows for Your Home
The Home Improvement Guide
ISBN-13: 978-1982091507

How to Buy Replacement Windows for Your
Home
The Home Improvement Guide
ISBN-13: 978-1495257582

House Windows Vocabulary
A Glossary of Definitions
ISBN-13: 9781984126399

Math Tables You Need
Go-To Solutions
ISBN-13: 978-1986944939